Brown Son of Lorca

A Boy Reclaimed in Poems,
Stories & Voice

Rodolfo Alvarado

Caballo Press of Ann Arbor

Ann Arbor, Michigan

Caballo Press of Ann Arbor
Copyright © 2025 by Rodolfo Valier Alvarado
All rights reserved

No part of this publication may be reproduced, distributed, or transmitted in any form or by any means, including photocopying, recording, or other electronic or mechanical methods, without the prior written permission of the publisher, except in the case of brief quotations embodied in critical reviews and certain other noncommercial uses permitted by copyright law.

For permission requests, please contact:
Caballo Press of Ann Arbor
admin@caballomediaproductions.com

Printed in the United States of America
on acid-free, archival-quality paper.
Typeset in Garamond and Avenir Next LT Pro

ISBN: 979-889766004-9

Cover design and interior layout inspired by the surrealist aesthetics of Salvador Dalí. Final composition and visual direction curated in collaboration with the author.

The first public performance of *To Speak What Was Buried* and a reading of the poems in this collection were presented by the author at La Nacional in New York City on June 9, 2025, during Danisarte's tribute to Federico García Lorca. Founded by renowned actress Alicia Kaplan, Danisarte champions diverse voices and original work.

--First Edition--

For my wife, Sonya, who saved me
from myself.

For my mother, Cruz, who gave me
her strength and her silence.

For Dennis, my stepfather, who built the walls that
sheltered my beginnings.

For my sister, Carolina, whose love never wavers,
whose belief never bends.

For Bidal Aguero, who often told me,
"Don't forget where you came from."

For Alicia Kaplan, for inviting a brown boy
from Lubbock to read and perform
his work in New York City.

And for Lubbock, Texas—
my first world, my forever root—
where memory lives in wind and sun,
and where the boy I first dreamed
of becoming breathed his first.

canción del naranjo seco
   (a Carmen Morales)

   Leñador.
   Córtame la sombra.
   Líbrame del suplicio
   de verme sin toronjas.

   ¿Por qué nací entre espejos?
   El día me da vueltas.
   Y la noche me copia
   en todas sus estrellas.

   Quiero vivir sin verme.
   Y hormigas y vilanos,
   soñaré que son mis
   hojas y mis pájaros.

   Leñador.
   Córtame la sombra.
   Líbrame del suplicio
   de verme sin toronjas.

         —Federico García Lorca, 1921

Table of Contents

Introduction... i

Poems

when we scream your name, Federico
    (an invitation/an invocation)............................ 1

found in the back, where they keep the ghosts....... 3

things I never told my step-father
    (Lorca did)... 6

Performance Piece

To Speak What Was Buried
    (A Performed Response)............................ 11

Short Stories

The Tongue I Was Told to Cut........................... 17

when I write with a white mind.......................... 21

Brown Son of Lorca.. 27

Introduction

My mother did not finish school. She made it as far as third grade. But she knew what this country asked of her son. She told me to lose my Spanish—my accent, my tongue. "If you're going to make something of yourself," she said, "you have to speak like them." And I did. I learned quickly. My teachers praised me. I became their brightest student. My mother believed in me, in my future. She was proud, even as she helped erase the part of me that spoke with her voice.

My mother ran a secondhand store established by my stepfather, Dennis, on the northeast corner of 19th Street and Avenue H in Lubbock, Texas. The store was called Dennis Trading Post. There was no apostrophe "s" after the "s" to mark possession, perhaps because it belonged more to my mother than to him. I spent my childhood there—surrounded by broken clocks, cast-off clothes, shoes, appliances, furniture, costume jewelry, cameras, war medals, and books. So many books. Books no one wanted. Books that whispered about lives far from the cotton fields and winds of West Texas.

One day, while on the verge of losing touch with the written and spoken Spanish language, I was sorting through a box in the back when I found a book of poems by Federico García Lorca. I didn't know who he was—but his words were unlike anything I'd ever read.

They were new.

Long.

Lyrical.

Beautiful.

Dangerous.

My stepfather—or perhaps it was me—saw the book in my hands and grew uneasy. "That book, by that so-called man, is not the kind of thing a boy should be reading," he muttered. He didn't mean poetry. He meant Lorca.

Lorca was not the father who raised me. But in many ways, he became the father who formed me. He—and those like him, writers with names like his—taught me how to see the world. Not just to look at it, but to question it. To wonder not only where I came from, but who I was becoming.

This book is my first attempt at answering those questions and to give shape to the silence that raised me.

I would forget about Lorca's book of poetry for years, even so, there were others—writers whose names, like Lorca's, sounded like echoes of my own—

Anaya,

García Márquez,

de Cervantes.

Allende.

Cisneros.

They found their way to me as a boy and in college, where they were often hidden in the back corners of the university library, like something the institution wasn't proud to own. When I opened those books as a young scholar, they reminded me of the Trading Post. I remembered the boy who used to hide at the back of the store with these books in his lap, more comfortable in someone else's story than in his own.

But it wasn't until I returned to Lubbock—after thirty years away—that the silence really broke.

I had returned to visit my sister, Carolina, and to perform a monodrama I had written about Anthony Acevedo—a World War II medic who, urged those around him to break their silence. The piece, which I began six years earlier, gave rise to much of what is contained in these pages: reclaimed stories, once buried, now spoken.

Stopping by where Dennis Trading Post once stood, I saw it was gone—paved over. In its place: a parking lot, just across the alley from what is now the Buddy Holly memorial. As I stood there, the air shifted. I could see it all again—the place we once called home: the towering warehouse in back, covered in corrugated tin; the white appliances lined up out front; the leaning bookshelves inside; the musty smell of clothes; the weight of memories still lingering in the air. My mother's voice calling me to help carry something, to help a customer. And then, for a moment, the boy I had been flickered back into being. And I felt him asking: "Where did you go?"

What you are about to read is an attempt to answer that question. It is part fact, part memory, part longing—and part fiction. I no longer know where one ends and the other begins, that's why the book's cover is inspired by Salvador Dalí, the surrealist painter and close companion (some say lover) of Lorca. Like Lorca's poems, Dalí's paintings exist in that blurred space between the known and the felt, the seen and the imagined. This book lives in that space too.

It is not a memoir. It is not entirely poetry or prose. It is not just story or performance. It is something else: a reclaiming. A reaching back through the silences that shaped me, to reclaim the boy I once was.

The poems, stories, and performance piece that follow are fragments of that reclamation. They are voices long buried, dreams revisited, and questions still echoing.

In the poems—*when we scream your name, Federico (an invitation/an invocation), found in the back where they keep the ghosts,* and *things I never told my step-*

father (Lorca did)—I explore what it means to inherit silence, to speak into the spaces where my voice was once denied, and to challenge the legacy of shame that came with being "different." In the performance piece, *To Speak What Was Buried*, I give breath to what had no name—what had to live, for too long, in the shadows of my throat.

The short stories are no less personal. In *The Tongue I Was Told to Cut*, I revisit the mother who loved me so fiercely she believed she had to erase me. In *when I write with a white mind*, I confront the duality I was taught to perform. And in *Brown Son of Lorca*, I return one last time to Dennis Trading Post and the boy I left behind—asking if he still remembers me, and whether I've earned the right to remember him.

These pieces do not offer answers. But they honor the questions. They reclaim the voice that was once corrected. The accent that was once shamed. The language that still lives beneath my breath, waiting to be called home.

And yes, you may notice—the Spanish in these pages comes sparingly. It arrives hesitantly, softly, and never fully returns. That, too, is intentional. Not because I don't love the language. But because this is where I am. This is the truth of a voice trying to reclaim what was stripped away.

I could have paid someone to translate the poems, to give you a version of me more fluent, more polished.

But that would not be true. Not to who I am now. Not to where I am in this journey of reclamation.

This collection is not the work of someone who has mastered Spanish. It is the work of someone finding his way back to it. Word by word. Breath by breath. Back to that little brown boy at the back of the store, sounding out syllables no one told him were sacred.

Perhaps one day I'll write a book entirely in Spanish.

We shall see.

Time is fleeting.

Can a life be reclaimed in words?

I hope so.

I pray so.

Rodolfo Alvarado
April 30, 2025
Ypsilanti, MI

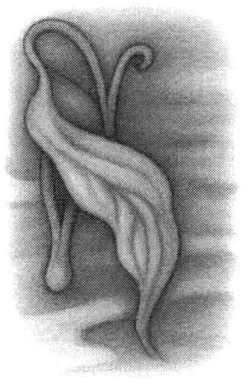

Poems

when we scream your name, Federico
(an invitation/an invocation)

they said your poems were pretty
until they realized they bled.

until they saw
you weren't writing metáforas—
you were writing yourself
into an open grave
you didn't dig
but already knew.

your name?
left off their syllabi.
your loves?
scratched out with a bureaucrat's pen.
your death?
called "uncertain"
so no one had to admit
what bullets do to beauty.

but here—Federico—
we invite you—
invoke you—
not in marble,
but in sweat,
and border crossings,
y cocinas del barrio,
where your verses

still catch in the throats
of niños y niñas who know
what it is to fear
their own bocas.

you were never just Spain.
you were brown skin y sombra,
hidden in a queer sun,
too dangerous to survive,
too honest to be forgotten.

so we invite—
invoke—
 your fantasma
into this room.
ask it to stand with ours.
share our microphone.

you don't get canonized, Federico—
you get heard—
you get spoken—
just like you meant it to be.

and this time,
we don't whisper your name,
we suck in the air
of your past
and our present
y lo gritamos,
"¡Federico!"

found in the back, where they keep the ghosts

i was just
a brown boy from Lubbock, Texas,
who didn't know
how to name what he felt—
only that it didn't fit
in cowboy boots,
or church pews
or locker rooms
where…
elementary school aged boys
stood naked.

i rediscovered you, Federico,
in the back of the university library—
where the light flickered
and the books were all in español,
donde no one ever went.

your name wasn't never mentioned.
your picture wasn't on any wall.
but there you were—
your pages
soft
waiting for me to find them.

i'd forgotten how men could write
like that.
about wounds that sing.
about love that hides.

about being too much and not enough
in the same skin.

you saved me.
made me stop hiding
at least for a while.

it took me some forty-five years—
to find you again.

to write,
not because the world asked me,
but because—like you—it didn't.

to perform
because i must,
not because i fear a theatre half-empty.

i speak
because you reminded me
of the journey
being about me—
not "them."

i am,
now
becoming
what i was made to erase.

i am because of you—
of a memory of you—

born when I was a boy.

your words—my words,
once buried,
are blooming again—
and again—

en mí.

things i never told my step-father (Lorca did)

you said poetry was fine
until it softened my voice.
until it brought men like him
into our house made of tin—
in books.
in language.
in emotion.
en mí.

"you don't read him," you said.
"that so-called man, he isn't right."

In your mouth,
"right,"
meant
not man enough.

so I kept him
hidden—
quiet
in the folds of a notebook
quiet.
beneath math homework
quiet—
always
quiet.

I read Federico
with the light turned low

so you wouldn't see
your step-son learning how to love
what you were taught
to fear.

Lorca taught me
what you never said—
that silence
is not protection.
it's punishment.

you raised me to be
tough.
stoic.
hard working.
not soft like verse,
not bright like the moon—
the kind "that so-called man,"
wrote into every wound.

pero my step-father,
beneath it all—
the love,
the pride,
the yelling,
the drinking—
I think you, too, were afraid.

we are the same
under the skin.

ripped away—
muscle.
blood.
bone.
and in the end,
our bodies and souls
lie in the same unmarked grave
as his—
that, *"so-called man,"*
never found,
but always...

felt.

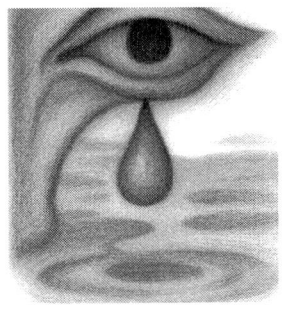

Performance Piece

To Speak What Was Buried
(A Performed Response)

(*Lights rise slowly. The performer is alone. A coat—maybe Lorca's style—hangs nearby. A shadow of history is present, but this is now. This is always now.*)

You want to know what it feels like?

To stand here…
to wear a man's name in your mouth—
not as a máscara,
but as a mirror?

To say "Lorca"
and feel the air tighten in your throat,
because somewhere between
his words and mine,
someone still wants both of us
to shut the hell up.

(*Beat. He walks downstage.*)

I did not come here to be polite.
I came here
to speak what's been buried.

Not resurrected—no.
This is not a ghost story.
This is a reckoning.
This is what happens when you give a dead poeta

a living body.

(*He touches his chest.*)

Mi cuerpo.
This one.
Brown.
From Lubbock, Tejas.
Straight-thinking,
but never small-minded.
Sí–yo.

The one who found Lorca
in a box,
in a language he was told
wasn't worth speaking,
because it wasn't white enough,
wasn't safe enough,
American-oh enough.

(*Steps forward. Stronger.*)

And now...
I carry his verses in my veins.
I say the things he never could.
I sing the names he wasn't allowed to write:

Dalí, whose name curled like smoke
in the margins of a love not spoken—
painted silence, never kissed.

Rapún, whose hands once held his heart

in the heat of backstage shadows—
buried in war, and still unnamed in print.

The dark boys of el callejón,
who wore moonlight like cologne,
whose laughter could've been poems,
had ink not feared their skin.

And all the vanished—the laborers,
the gypsies, los negros en Harlem—
whose names were too brown, too broke,
too bold to pass a censor's blade.

I dance with the duende,
not as metaphor—
but as survival.

Because every time I perform,
I refuse to disappear.

(*Beat. He removes the coat from its hook. Holds it.*)

You want to know what it feels like?

It feels like walking onstage
with centuries on your shoulders—
still choosing
to open your mouth.

To speak the unspeakable.
To name yourself.

To name him.
And to not apologize
for either.

(*Lights begin to fade.*)

Because shutting up
is no longer an option.

Not for me.

Not for you.

Not for those who stand
with Federic... oh.

(*Blackout.*)

Short Stories

The Tongue I Was Told to Cut

There is a violence that does not bruise, but it lingers.

It sits beneath the tongue, beneath the skin, waiting.

My mother called it love.

When I was a boy in Lubbock, Texas, she forbade me from speaking Spanish at home.

"No te van a tomar en serio," she said. "They won't take you seriously. You have to lose that accent if you want to be someone."

She didn't say "they" meant white people. She didn't have to.

So I practiced. I practiced until my "r"s no longer rolled, until my vowels stretched long and flat.

Until my tongue forgot what it meant to be soft.

I burned.

And I stayed quiet.

I wonder sometimes if Lorca would have understood.

A brown boy made to silence half his voice.

A boy raised in a land where Spanish was a shame to be scrubbed away, not a canción to be sung.

Lorca, who spoke his truth in a Spain that told him to hide.

Who wrote of blood, of tierra, of the unspeakable, in a language that was his rebellion.

In my house, silence was safety.

My mother believed the world was too small for a brown boy with an accent.

At school, I was praised for my English. For my neatness. For how well I could pass.

But among my classmates—those who still spoke Spanish freely—I was "el otro"—"the other."

They teased me when I tried. When my words stumbled. When I couldn't remember the names for things that had no English in my mouth.

I learned to smile, to laugh it off.

But I carried the shame in my chest like a secret weight.

And now, as un hombre, I still carry it.

In rooms where Spanish fills the air like música, I hesitate.

I reach for words I know but don't trust.

I fear being found out: "No eres de aquí, ni de allá."

Lorca once fled to New York, seeking a place where he could breathe outside the suffocation of Spain.

But even there, he found isolation.

He wrote of Harlem, of towers, of the machines that devour the soul.

I too ran—to escape the suffocation of Lubbock, to escape the language, to escape those who reminded me I couldn't speak it well enough.

And yet—even now—especially in New York—the language finds me.

In Central Park, Battery Park, Times Square, Washington Square.

Street vendors, shop owners, abuelitas on benches.

They speak it. They sing it. And I whisper to myself: "Puedes correr, pero el idioma te encuentra, ¿verdad? Como un fantasma."

I spent years avoiding Spanish.

I read Lorca in translation, afraid of misunderstanding him.

Afraid of mispronouncing myself.

His words came filtered through someone else's voice—still powerful, but not whole.

Lorca taught me the price of silence is too high.

He wrote, "The duende... does not come at all unless he sees that death is possible."

And for us—boys and girls like me—death is not metaphor.

It lives in the corners of our mouths. In what we are told to erase. But duende came. And with it, not death, but the need to speak.

Now, when I read Lorca, I read him in Spanish. Not always aloud. Not always confidently. But I read him. Because truth isn't in perfection. It's in the struggle to claim what was taken.

I may never speak Spanish the way I was meant to.

But Lorca was willing to die for his truth.

For his voice.

So why—

Why ain't I?

when I write with a white mind

There are two minds in me when I write.

One learned to sharpen its words like clean knives—precise, polished, safe.

That mind came from my mother. From her fear, wrapped in love.

From her dream that I could be more if I were less of what I was.

The other mind is older. Más salvaje.

(sahl-VAH-heh: meaning, wilder).

It stumbles, breaks rules, doesn't care for grammar or grace.

It writes like it bleeds.

It doesn't ask permission.

That mind came from la raza she didn't want me to be.

I didn't know I was switching between them, not at first. I thought I was just refining. I thought I was getting better.

But now I see it.

When I write with a white mind, I explain.

I ask the reader to accept me, to see that I am educated, measured, reasonable.

I try not to take up too much space.

When I write with a brown mind, I dare.

I don't explain.

I show.

Y lloro.

I spill, let the words run wild, como caballos sueltos—like they've waited too long to be free.

I take as much space as I need.

My mother didn't mean harm.

She wanted me to survive.

So she gave me English like a sword and told me to cut.

"Speak properly," she said.

"Don't let them think you're some cholo."

She ironed my shirts, combed my hair flat. Made me look like someone I didn't recognize.

"Smile," she said.

"Show them your white, straight teeth."

"Show them you're better."

And I was.

Better.

But not whole.

When I write now, I can feel it—the shift. There is a moment when the words start to feel false. When I have to stop, breathe, and ask myself:

"Who is writing this?

¿Soy yo?

Or the boy my mother built from fear?"

Lorca knew this split. He lived between worlds—public and private, poeta y hombre—someone who could not name his love aloud.

He wrote, "No todos dormimos por la noche. Algunos tenemos que mantenernos despiertos para ver cómo el mundo llora sus lágrimas silenciosas."

I'd been asleep too long.

My awakening… it happened in a poem. I didn't know I was writing it wrong, not at first.

I thought I was being careful, clear. Doing what a writer is supposed to do.

I sat at my desk, the light dim, the page half-full, and I read it back.

It was perfect.

Polished.

Safe.

Muerto.

The poem was about my grandfather. About the fields he worked—the five acres he owned—the songs he sang.

But I had stripped him bare. I wrote him like an idea, not a man. I took out the polvo, the sweat, the Spanish. I wrote him as if he belonged in a book for people who never knew men like him.

And I hated it.

I crossed it out.

Line by line.

Then I wrote—without thinking:

When I write with a white mind,

I am not myself.

I fear my own tongue,

the curve of my words,

the shame of a rolling "r",

the weight of a mother's eyes.

I explain. I apologize.

I cut my voice clean.

I bleach my blood

for the approval of those

who taught me how

to play the game.

When I write with a brown mind,

yo lloro.

I scream.

I spill.

I love my broken Spanish,

my crooked truths,

my rolling r-r-r-r-s,

mis fantasmas.

When I write with a brown mind,

soy completo.

When I read the poem back, I wept.

Because I knew—supe—

what?

¿ah quién?

Yo.

Lorca was killed for what he could not hide. For the man he refused to erase. And here I was, erasing myself. Line by line.

No más.

Now, I write with my sangre—

pure—

unbleached.

With the silence of my abuelito's hands, and the noise of every word my mother told me not to say.

I write with a brown mind,

as a brown son of Lorca.

I write

as me.

Brown Son of Lorca

Before I knew what I was becoming, I was just a boy in a store full of other people's stories.

My mother called it a trading post—a secondhand store. A place where belongings passed from the firsthand to the second. Cameras that no longer captured. Shoes that no longer fit. Military jackets with patches from wars I'd never heard of.

She bought them cheap from people who needed money more than memories. She sold them to others who thought they still had use.

Those with turned-up noses called what we sold junk.

But I didn't see junk. I saw secrets—secretos.

There was a corner in the back where the light didn't quite reach. That's where I hid. With the books no one wanted—manuals, old Bibles, cookbooks with missing pages. I'd sit on a crate and read, and for a little while, I wasn't just the boy in the shop.

I was somewhere else.

One day, under a stack of yellowed newspapers, I found a book with a green cloth cover. The title was strange. The letters danced—"Federico García Lorca. *Romancero Gitano.*"

I didn't know what it meant. But I opened it anyway.

I didn't understand the words, not at first.

But something about them moved. Like the West Texas wind in a cotton field—you can't see it, but you feel it.

The first line I read was:

"Verde que te quiero verde."

"Green, how I love you green."

I didn't know what it meant. But I read it again.

And again.

And each time, it felt like a door opened—not in the store, not in the pages, but somewhere inside me.

I sat there for hours, el libro heavy in my hands.

My mother called me from the front of the store, but I didn't answer.

I wasn't there anymore.

I was with Lorca.

With his green nights. With his guitars that weep. With his silences that screamed.

Around me, the store whispered.

The cameras watched.

The shoes waited.

The military jackets hung like soldiers still standing guard.

I wondered who they belonged to?

Who had taken the photos?

Who had stumbled in those shoes?

Who had worn the jacket with medals, or the necklace now tarnished and forgotten?

And more than that—where did I belong?

Was I just the boy who cleaned the shelves, counted change, was told to speak better, be better?

Or was I something else?

Was I the thing my friends called me? The coconut—"Brown on the outside, white on the inside."

Or "el profesor"—the one who always had the answers, the one the teachers praised, the one who didn't talk like them anymore—and perhaps—never did.

I laughed with them. I let them joke.

But I felt it.

The space growing between me and the boy I had been.

Lorca didn't laugh.

His poems didn't laugh.

They sang. They died. Lloraban.

And in that moment, I didn't want to laugh either.

I wanted to scream, yell: "¿Quién soy yo?"

Not to my mother. Not to my friends. Not even to the teachers who smiled at me like I was some prize.

But to myself.

After I found Lorca's book, I saw the store differently.

It wasn't just a place where people sold their pasts.

It was a place where I was losing mine.

The cameras sat still on the shelves, but I thought: Why were there so few photos of us? No snapshots of birthdays. No framed holidays. No pictures of my mother bent over her sewing machine, or of me lacing up my shoes beneath the orange-pink sky of Lubbock. We sold cameras to strangers, but never seemed to keep one long enough to capture our own story.

The shoes, too, sat still—lined up along the walls. And I thought: Why did mine always have to shine? Why did my mother scrub them until they looked like they'd never touched dirt—like I wasn't from where we were from?

And the books—those broken books—stacked in boxes like tombstones lying flat. They weren't just stories; they were warnings. Warnings of what dies when you're told to become someone else.

I kept Lorca's book hidden.

Not because I was afraid my mamá would take it.

But because I didn't want her to tell me it didn't matter.

That it was just poetry. Just words. Just a book—and in Spanish.

It was mine.

The book—his words.

For the first time, something secondhand felt like mine.

One afternoon, I sat in the back, reading his words aloud to myself.

Trying to sound out the Spanish my mother had long since washed from my mouth with soap. My tongue stumbling, but still trying—tratando—to romance the moon, like Lorca.

"El... nee-nyoh... la... mee-rah..., mee-rah....

El... nee-nyoh... la... ehs-tah... me-rahr-do...."

The boy looks at her, looks.

The boy is looking at her.

I didn't know who she was.

But I felt like I was looking, too.

At the past.

At myself.

At the words in my first-grade reader:

"*See Jane run,*

See Dick run,

Run. Run. Run"

Looking at the brown boy I was—slipping away.

Becoming the new me—the original—erased.

I still remember the way the store smelled—of old leather, dust, and something sweet I could never name.

I remember the way my mamá smiled when I spoke English just right.

And I remember how my heart beat faster each time I opened that green book—*before*.

Before his language and self were taken away from me.

Before I knew the price of forgetting.

I read words meant for someone like the boy I used to be.

I am the son of the woman who wanted me to survive.

I am the son of a store full of forgotten things.

I am the Brown Son of Lorca.

But I didn't know it then.

Not yet.

I stood at the edge of a life I couldn't yet see, holding a book I no longer fully understood, in a world that would soon begin to complete me—
to shape me into someone my little brown self could never be.

I didn't know I would leave him behind—
the boy in the back of the store,
the boy who wondered,
who read Lorca like a secret prayer.

And now, I fight.

I fight, with all that's left in this old man—este viejito—
to find him again.

To find his voice.

To find the language that was taken from us both.

The store is gone now.

The cameras, the shoes, the uniforms, the books—sold, tossed, lost.

Scattered in the wind, buried in the dump, their stories silenced.

Only Lorca would know how to speak of their scattering—of how we become polvo, and how the West Texas dust still carries the breath of what was.

I look around me now, at the things I've kept.

A book.

A photograph.

A name.

And I wonder—

Someday, will these too end up in the hands of someone second?

Someone who does not know where they came from?

Will someone hold them, as I once held that green book, and wonder?

Or will these things end up in a dump?

I don't know.

But I write.

Porque tengo que hacerlo.

Because some things, even if lost, still deserve to be reclaimed—to be remembered.

Because soft—but defiant—is the only way I know now.

And it is the way, I believe—

Lorca, if he was my father—

oh, if he was my father—

would have wanted

his brown son

to be.

About the Author

Rodolfo Alvarado is an award-winning eclectic writer, scholar, and performer. His poems and performance piece from this collection were first presented in New York City at La Nacional, as part of Danisarte's tribute to Federico García Lorca. Later that same year, he was selected to perform his acclaimed solo play Undesirable Secrets—based on the life of Holocaust survivor Anthony Acevedo—on an Off-Broadway stage as part of the 2025 United Solo Theatre Festival and at Theatre for the New City's Dream Up Festival, both in New York City.

A native of Lubbock, Texas, Alvarado is making peace with the fact the he must draw on his roots to explore themes of silence, identity, and cultural reclamation. He holds a Ph.D. in Fine Arts, an MFA in Playwriting from Texas Tech University, and an MA in History from Eastern Michigan University, where he was a Parks/King/Chávez Fellow and a University Fellow.

His biography *The Untold Story of Joe Hernandez: The Voice of Santa Anita* received the Dr. Tony Ryan Book Award, and he was named an Emerging Latino Author by *The Latino Book Review*. His work has been published by the University of Michigan Press, Michigan State University Press, Arte Público Press, Alpha Books of New York, and Caballo Press of Ann Arbor, among others.

He lives and writes in Michigan. To learn more, visit: www.rodolfoalvarado.com

Made in the USA
Columbia, SC
12 June 2025